AF483537

ISBN:
ISBN-13: 979-8-9895598-0-0

1st edition, December 2023

A,

(conversance)

the writings are one person's sense for understanding,
creative amalgamations drawn from nature and the world
at large.
nothing is for everyone and one's own ideas change over
time. a willingness to be open, not seeking to become
entrenched.

the mind is endless, limitless
you can find yourself through it or lose yourself in it

humility and honesty to understand if this is the time.
if the words tell but do not reach, softening edges, fear not
for reaching out. tuition is near and the world is full of
love

~ SES

Spring Awakening

Sceen was young once upon a time. He entered
consciousness of mind, awareness of self, loss of ignorance
and the birth of knowledge. New world beginnings flowed
into the acquisition of memory, the laying down of history,
the unfolding thenceforth of perpetual happenstance.
Dreams coming true and the creation of new dreams.
It began with expressions of optimism and hope, an
openness of belief that every coming moment can paint
the world with the richness of life's treasures, the
mundane and the supernatural.
Love of language, a flood of emotions and teaching
understandings, beyond all thought, action.

polychromatic color waves wash over days spent in lucid
beauty, seeking cosmic liaisons to journey, trade lessons
and share time with. the best things in life are free.

lyrical movements painting landscapes in the mind,
bubble pop magentas and first layer indigos spacing vivid
angles, seven dimensions twisting wildstyle graffiti

Educations came from mixtapes and nights on desolate
beaches, thunderstorms lighting up distant night skies,
darkness wiping out the horizon off shore.
look, you can't tell where the sky ends and the ocean begins..

Suddenly the lights came on and everything was
everywhere. First explorations of a busy, busy mind.
Garrulous tendencies in the presence of love. Reaching
across abysses with soliloquies that syncretized all the
idealism hidden by a heartbreaking world.

Spring green fields and plasticity windows. You can be
anything, even yourself.

So many words for what has transpired in so little a time.
Not yet a young man, now pray tell, whatever could all the
fuss be about.

Every circumstance every philosophy every truth.
Historical, contemporary, impressionistic. Post modern,
abstract.
Without shells of personal narratives and without
confinement, opening surprising and teaching.

Experience, error, assent and synthesis. The inertia of
logic trenching out new pathways. Trying to understand.
Making sense.

The world starts calling and keeps calling. One's place in it
all.

Boundaries and relationships intertwined from so many
years ago, lenses that overlay and uncovered a
confounding acceptance through the years.

loss
Things changed everything changed. Who am I what is
the world what is life what is real. Ways of knowing that
lose their way in time.

When you carry innocence you may not know it, until you
can look back and see how things are different now from
how they were back then.

There were stories of morose and melancholy worldwide,
the comfortable stare of feeling down, an unpleasantness
about self awareness blending too closely with self
consciousness.
Yes there were stories to be told but much of the real
tragedies of life had been kept from consumptive
awareness, fortunate to experience magic in childhood
before a man found himself on the other side, with
everyone who knew what he knew.
A banality of tortured and endless moments endured
through the lucidity of loss, that's what's real.
One things ends another immediately begins. Brace
yourself, and welcome to a new world, a new life.

striving through dark times that couldn't hold the colors,
awash in slate grays
   lost   dissoci ated   alienated

An old soul opened anew with the thawing of the earth.
The first step of the rest of his life.
No looking back now, this is happening, one way or the
other. Can hardly believe it but it's true.

whispers rushed the ocean air across his body
I can see you

what was already on its way

slovenly spellbound, a barren emptiness with nascent
perceptions of disappearing faith,
another way

shapeshifting fractal vortexes subsume
primrose protean pythagorean progressions

a moment can last forever when you're in it

Foundations

mind states

at home with the feel of water
floating, drifting with the current. time passes, lose the
feeling of sand underneath. in deep waters can't reach it
but know it's there, an understanding until the storm
passes and one can take root in the ground again.

I

Stay awake. Don't stay asleep. Make it all happen before
you're six feet deep.
Don't forget. Always remember. Learn even just one thing.
Know something, understand something, change
something.

Nothing to fear, nowhere to hide. Don't try to avoid death
by avoiding life.

Beyond the ho hum lie soulful yearnings and mortal
implications, existential considerations, and
environmental and cultural devastations.

II

The onset of tension and better dismissed emotions that tinge everything with a feeling that something is wrong. That it would be much better if something else was happening, anything but what is.
Those feelings, like all others, can't be denied. Things may not be looking good, at all. It's fine, go into safe chambers with the understanding that there is not anything of you, from you or to you that is not for you. An allowance to listen, to feel it through, guiding into a new place, a better space.

we always make it don't we?

III

a problem?

Words formulate thoughts and feelings that can be easy to
believe in, influencing states of mind that create
biochemical conditions in mindbody as soon as they are
introduced. They create the world one steps into. They
matter.

Waves and vibrations passing through each other, even if it
can't be seen, it's happening.

Can't see them can't hardly imagine them yet anything to
everything can most definitely *feel* them. In out and
through in a seamless flow, join up with the other energies
in a universal super flow

Time puts boundaries on the connections between
destruction and creation, can't get caught looking back.

partitions of matter and dimensional understanding create
many where there is only One

IV

time invested into undoing learned ways and
remembering the things he could never be without, then
the problems stopped pretending. obstacles shifted into
opportunities.

cannot be one side without others, all depends where one
is looking.
how many can there be, all the ways light shines through
the faceted jewels of life

how many angles do waves and vibrations have

allow things to open up and come to the surface. let time
rest and come back to it. see it again and new sides appear,
a new perspective, a new reality.

High gloss outlines and color crush hieroglyphics moving
4D letters in space on an eye candy top to bottom, just
around the corner from the rescue mission. Three palm
trees waved with the breeze in front of the lot across the
street.

Mahogany seaweed wilted in the afternoon sun as the east
African tide rolled out into the Indian Ocean. Feather
light leaves wafted in the air of a small courtyard a short
walk up from the sand. A soft underlit space four feet
below the canopy of a grand Red Royal Poinciana, a green
parrot rests its wings.
Felt calm in the dappled shade, another heaven sent day
milling about with a chancey love of life.

V

Living performances and expressions of self, beautiful amazing. Incessant distractions make it easy to drop gratitude for the dead weight of attachments, that's casual madness.

Memories stretched across the canvas, laid down in thick oils, blending brushstrokes with experience. Coalescence as time passes and the paint dries. New colors, new overlays, subsumption.

VI

See the sights horizon where sky blue meets ocean blue. Look up, see the mountain top. Start climbing, keep climbing. Trials, tests, tribulations. Blood sweat and tears. Finally, at the top. Take a look around and *breathe it in, oxygen. Oxygen* is persistence and truth that has been floating around dark matter for millions of years. Come to move around the body for a while, an exchange for carbon that is sent back to the tree.
Who knew it would all happen like that, ending up here, now, like this.
Sea hawk swoops over shoulder and takes aim at a school of glimmer fish in the water below. Exhale. The view opens wider, see the top of this mountain is the base of another. Keep moving. Keep rising.

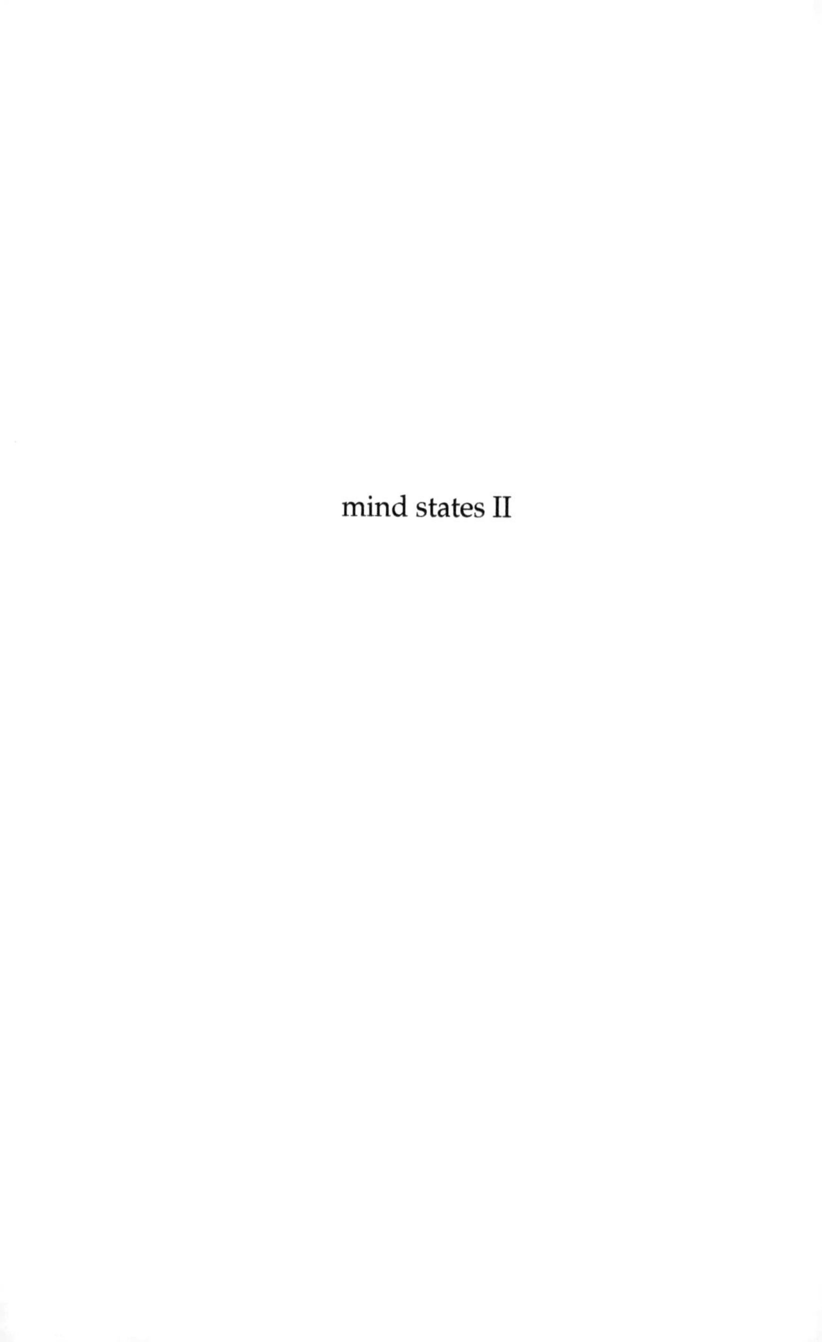

mind states II

this is the place

A joyous spring, a happy summer, a comforting fall and an
early winter. Seasons changed and back into the spring of
life, Sceen only beginning to understand the power of
conscious expression. One realization that took a decade
to grasp expressed in one sentence and nine seconds.
Awareness, the first step.

I

deadline apprehensions seized by the fruition of
consequences lying in wait. what if. trepidation snowballs
rush down with packets of powder popping steam, makes
it seem like it's coming on faster than it is. the speed of a
moment is all that one has to keep up with, that one can.

Get there once. Once is forever.

II

when you're there, not a moment before.

there is time but don't be fooled by holidays, every second counts. eons and epochs lay a trillion traces, focus remains with current matters in hand.

without conflicting opposition shift and flow in the Know

III

casting stories up ahead before getting there, then seeing. does it have to be the grays of woebegone visions and the morose façade of eventuality. no, doesn't have to.

everyone worries about creating the future but can you predict the present.

IV

Things that affect mindbody affect the mind and the body. Filling tranquil spaces of mind with heavy confusion creates tension and breaks symmetries, taking away from the regenerative power and peaceful grace of the body. The mind can be tricked with self deluded pretense and affirmation, but not the body.

Things oftentimes don't live up to the dreadful pageantry
of what might be, an empty romance with sentimentality,
self pity and fantasy.

Stay here because when you get there and the experience
wasn't as you had imagined then all the time pretending
and playing, dropping into self vicarious and vapid retreats
of those low, hollow spaces will be revealed as time that's
been wasted. Gone.

V

—at this moment the most important thing to remember is
that you know how to *slow down.* use your knowledge,
slow it down and create pictures instead of words.

when a break is needed carve out peace for the next day,
no matter what is happening.

VI

What's around the next corner, don't know and can't know,
that's what life taught him.
Prepare for everything be ready for anything. (*anything?*)
Still, surprises bewildered, like a baby seeing jack-in-the-
box popping into reality for the first time again, a joyful
expression of mindful presence without the glare of
anticipation and memory.
A five-year-old captures more vivid imagination because
life long unlearning hasn't yet commenced.

VII

Making things up as one goes along, why not unparallel.
Evanescence, without the drag of leaden fields, talking
thinking reevaluating and pondering on and on and on.
All thought is prelude. *dream*

VIII

Sudden, momentous change arrives with tumult and
chaos. Absorb the impact, feel, yes the mind is embattled.

There won't be time later for metamorphic heartache so
keep accepting, then let it go. When it returns keep on and
keep patience. Patience is a virtue.

VIIII

angles are created by exponents of circular and elliptical
interplanetary movements
consonance

see something you hadn't seen before, was it always there
before you saw it. change the way you look at things then
the things you are looking at change. what changed.

yin and yang. the point where the two meet intersects with
life at the present moment. the balance of the indivisible
space where love and hate cannot coexist. the darkness
from the absence of light more grandiose than retinal
observations may conclude.

beyond divisions

no style

X

Keep the body still and move the mind around. Keep the
mind still and move the body around. As needed.

Laying atop retracting plateaus of transposing ocean, a
peaceful place where water laps up on the belly in the
center of a thrashing storm. Commotions atop the high
wire haywire, stillness at the core.

inner dynamic expressions always have a home

XI

Leave the outside forces on the outside, ricocheting off the laughter of a child parading at silly scamps clamoring for a way in through clear glass windows.

stay loose, keep it tight

thoughts without salutation
essential questions asked and answered without linguistic symbolism

meditate back to one

there is no before and after in the here and now

momentum cascades propel presence

a light heart grows bigger, opens boundless

in motion

I

The flows of spring. Renewal, rebirth, rejuvenation and
reciprocity. Days of rains and flowers. Free style
inspiration and graceful, heart first ways of living.

Mindbody. The relationship that sets the foundation for
everyone and everything. What lies within.

Striving for simple ways of being. Keeping the language
simple. Be simple. Mindless inventions like stories,
hesitation and wasted thought drift away. Knowing
without any need of mammalian logic.
universalflow

II

thought plan motivation execution success. what was
accomplished at what expense, what was learned and
what can be forgotten about. what carries on and what
will spark revealing through creativity.

simple things get pulled under by complication and
complicated things get intertwined. clamps of logistics,
time, present circumstances. the malaise of history and
tales of regret.

familiar foes and new invaders lying in wait, chomping at
the bit for openings created by fear and uncertainty,
rushing in, derailing flight into the center of the sun. stay
focused.
no suspense in it any more. easy to see, clear, but not
always easy to defend against.

III

what if this happens and what if so many things happen
like so many things that have happened. taking guesses
about which part of the water you are in.

what if an angle had been missed and the window for
swaying the unfolding of events closes, and then the future
becomes that past. what should have been done and what
could have been done suddenly becomes easier to pick
out.

back there in the made up nowhere, before it exists,
instead of being here. time burning both ends of the
candle.

hindsights of memories without immediacy and
forgiveness lay a heavy glaze of self doubt. reflection
weighed down with judgement to someone only deserving
of love.

released from attachment, more openings for acceptance.

IV

things continue to transpire and no room in the world that
created them for the requisite calm of mindful time.
where deep intelligence lies without making its evolution
felt. the spaces between the notes create the music.

pauses for emotions and peace at red lights. sinking
feelings and revelations on an empty subway car.
biochemical physiology that filters throughout the body,
back to the mind, to the body
the more quiet and still it is the more you can hear

V

coming down like world confusion. it rains it pours.
lifelong insecurity against the shine flowing out.

so much to deal with, will everything be ok. beyond the
fear of fate and all that has come to pass you know why,
always come through.

VI

the waves never stop for they may have no beginning and
no end, they carry energy, energy that can neither be
created nor destroyed, only transferred.

turquoise waters move across the sandbar, sea green light
under the sunless glow of a total eclipse

anything can happen and it will

VII

illusions of satiety and lure of forcefulness wreck inner
peace in a moment. a rush to react. an equal and opposite
reaction. getting caught up instead of swept up

life can lead to glory no matter the speed

when it seems the worst possible time to let go, let go.

VIII

gloom and doom are an opportunity to step back. answers
are easy enough to arrive at, don't forget to think of them.

at the destination   right now
and always will be

IX

So much to be grateful for, everything really.
Can't let bad days slip by with the mundaneness that
befalls modern existence. Get lulled into giving treasure
away for the idle busyness of production consumption.
Get used to how good things are, start looking around,
creating comparisons, inventing problems.

Getting everything done all the time at any expense. Mind
and body suffer. Soul is starved. Inspiration fades.
Meaning dissipates with the loss of gratitude.

Nitrogen and phosphorus seep into the water, particles
form in the air. Acid rain. Vitality gets drawn down, takes
time to dig out, takes time to get right.

X

18,000,000 miles happen so fast. new places new years
new seasons. can you believe it's already Friday can you
believe it's July. yes, I can.

The best days of life ran on, washing away numbing
shadows of city winter life, arcing in azure skies as spring
sunshine hit soft typing paper white petals.

then the best days didn't come around like they used to.
things change, then change again. it keeps happening.
losing the effort of keeping up with how the stories and
feelings are connected because now they're all connected,
they always were

Does it need to be so deliberate. flow is easy to know so
why all the thinking. thought is pretext in a place where
words don't exist.
time passes, less thinking, more doing, simplify down to
being.

A place where who you are and all there is to see is to be.

Every moment is the opportunity of a lifetime.

washing over, shaping and carving

  they never stop, not even when they reach shore

Beloved

New realities appear, find yourself in what couldn't be
imagined. Things will never be the same again again.
Permanent imprints and a disintegrated compass, trying to
come to terms with the fact that what was will never be
again.
Self empathy expressed through endless forgiveness,
because the word that means so much is survive.

rays of sunlight that broke through years of rain

all I have is my life

I

Unrepentant changes require moving past conclusions of
smartness and intellect. Logic is good sounding, in step
with the clockwork of the tick tock world. but does it feel
right
Beyond the fray of new age cages and old world
malevolence, to origins, before the serpent offered the
apple. Who he always was, who he *really*, *truly* is.
Detached from armors of culture and society. Loosened
from molded constitutionality, released from divergences
of disconnected and imaginary differences.

Tease apart the strands, everything that's happened since
the first cry.

Begin, and never lose sight that happiness is a reflection of
wellness, no matter what you see out there.

II

You are the creator, never forget that.

III

what stays what goes
No turning back. So Get Ready.   Get Set.   GO

sparks unveil, sun storms rise

seeing oneself poses how one got to be this way.
what was I thinking, was I thinking. what I was doing. was
I doing anything.
why did I try so hard to hold onto so many useless things
for so long.

Judgement and regret fill in, guilt begins siphoning off.
Guilt casts a web that draws in loved ones so they can
share in what hasn't been, of what should and could and
would but will not be. It feels like it's giving meaning to
the past but it's robbing one of the present and the future.

An amazing time to be alive but choose to spend it riding
joyless whims into places that don't exist, unless one
creates them.
Things you worked so hard for washing out with the tide.
Getting hard to see and things have gotten murky again.
Time fades as it clears.

Questions come fast and furious when things held deep
are brought to the surface, exposing the heart of the
matter.
Enjoy that gnarling grind of churlish regret and
reminiscence ten last times. The more it stings, the more is
being learned.
Step into open views. Find meanings inside adolescent
heartaches and bring peace to that person. Evolve
empathy for a life that's become too rich.

IV

Meeting unwanted expectations of anything or anyone
outside of, be it real or imagined, is a lazy order of living
that leads to psychic strife and physical affliction.
validate *yourself*

Whether you were aware at the time or not you created
yourself. You are creating yourself now and you always
will be.

From nothing come into being in that place and time with those people. Each with their own and to their own. Atoms, protons, strings. Gravity, constellations, solar system UNI VERSE

V

The concept of Home soared to prominence in the crest between the formative years and first entry into the flow. A child no longer, as layers, lenses and innate constitutions all started laying claim.

Awakened and forevermore impossible to unsee. Ignorance is bliss, but it is still ignorance. A seismic shift to remaining lucid, no matter the trials being self witnessed.

Make a way in the world and get an education. Learn something about yourself and understand something about life.

Boundaries are the most basic structures. All is one but if boundaries don't exist you don't exist. A naïve idealism can allow others to grow rooted and entrenched in a variety of things that cede to seductions. Wanting to be thought of well, to be useful. Wanting to please, always to please. Vanishing by externalizing, far far away from actualization. Wake up one day and wonder how you became invisible.

The world opens up, its beauty in kind with the experiences of life. Assurance grows beyond doubt, rooted in divine ground. Innocence fades and things get real. Mass distractions appear one day as the antipode to time spent in self evident wisdom. Incessant needs. To do things, to get things done. They quickly grow to balance simplicity and soon overtake. Minor entreaties begin to dominate. The equation reciprocates and the challenge becomes bringing it back to balance, maybe even to the way it was before. Time expensed venturing in and out.

Don't get in too deep, don't get trapped. Move away and stay away and no matter what keep it in its place.

See where you started now look how far you've gone. Are you gone, oh no, you're gone.

Beautiful soul, lying dormant behind the illusions. Growing in knowledge of self but still too quick to move according to worldly persuasions. So fast you can't see it, but can you feel it.
Time can't hold it, you're the only one that can break it.

Given to endless philosophy and theory when presence is the way. It begins when thoughts end. It starts when you're ready.

sights set

Balloons rise and candles light to celebrate life and the mother that gave birth to it. Eighteen million miles sojourned around the sun, the solar system shifted slightly with the movement of cosmos, gravity and mathematics. A backdrop of timeless primordial infinities, another victory lap in this thing called Life.
Every star in the night sky twinkles a pin hole through the mirrors of the universe. What can't be understood and may never be known.

Ambition realized some rewards, a little security, then the failure of success led the invisible lure of complacency in. Back to nothing. Inward and upward.

Ready to see yourself but can you. Reflection. The forever challenge to the self conscious organism, to see something from the outside when one is inside, the very thing one is attempting to observe.
How did things come to this and why. Mid evening wonders that overpowered with jade green auras in the moonlit afternoon.
The world is a mirror. Simple, easy. Can be. Only have to look. Reflections in nature and interpersonal relationships help one see but are you willing.

Personality is the way each person secures
interconnectedness with life and the world.

Honesty. Accuracy. The good and the bad. The
untenable, the lamentable. The joyous and the indifferent.
Don't look away, don't try to run away, from yourself, you
can't.

Want to be new but give in to the resistance of feeling new
things, of things one can't bear to feel. It cannot happen
that way, it will not. Everything is everything and
everything touches everything. The challenge inlay with
recompense.
Aspects of persona shaped by exterior wave dynamics
weigh down, obscure. Get caught up, held up, thrown
back. Let them things go and let yourself go.
If you don't know who you are how can others.

Sceen caught that first little glimpse, finally seeing beyond
the boredom of mindless meandering and too much of a
good thing.

Naturally inclined to introspect and internalize, a
heightened awareness of the connections between people
and environment, between all things.
How the energy changed when he walked in the room,
how the molecular makeup changed. What they feel and
how his expressions affect what transpires. Spaces
between people revealing glances and movement.

The balance of all aspects can elevate or pull down,
depending on the level of understanding and
nourishment, what is being fed and acknowledged.

Feed the faith, starve the doubt.

Insights veiled in the conceited veneer of self absorption
are devoured by the plague of plagues, self righteous
wisdom. Beware speaking it it may catch you.

Without inspiration the ego is at ease with the power to
affect people and things around it, to impose threats
without a care as to who or what. Whatever.
A moving target shifting with cloaks of distraction,
deception, diversion, illusion, projection.
now you see me now you don't

Attempts to see bring forth denial. A natural expectation.
Looking and thinking without consideration that it is
being seen out there because it resides within. Mirrors.
Reality exists to one's own vision yet there is only one
truth.

Practiced compositions and material world reflections guiding one to root causes of conflict. Slowly the things that aren't true fade away, murmurs quiet to a peace and you can see what it is you were so desperately trying to avoid looking at.

a story

Crossing one finish line after another. Hours, days and years that stretched into decades, time given to the labors of study, education and training. Sequential obstacle courses and endless arrays of stress, swarming skies like locust.
New hurdles appear as soon as old ones pass, dropping invisible weight that cements down like concrete. Suspension of a living system in constant states of tension and apprehension. A sympathetic nervous system that finds a new home above zero.

Holding ground the way he envisioned, not exceeding the personal costs of well being.

Can't forget that breaking promises to self leads to irreversible decisions that only become more expensive over time. Everything else is secondary and can be made up through gratitude and adaptation.

Conquest of a piece of paper that means something. Four years for the first diploma, a byproduct of good times and new explorations. Five years for the second, taking spiritual revolution many steps further and developing a professional style of discipline and learning. Four years more dedicated to the third. An overwhelming, onerous endeavor, like drinking all of the water coming out of a fire hydrant. No contemplation without experience.
A comma and two instant symbols that became the

acronym after the surname on a third piece of parchment.
Costs that reached extortionate levels. Sacrifice and
achievement that could never, be captured by a two letter
suffix or prefix.
Half a young life to endless rote memorization and
repetitious forgetting. Then came the beginning of
specialization and practical learning. Quicksand traps
made easy for perfectionism. The toil of low wage labor in
a domineering and inhuman system that was bad for the
mind and bad for the body. Suffused with self affected
proclamations about the way things have always been
done. Willful and heartless ignorance from a well spoken,
gutless intellectual.
Five years more for the final piece and all in all fifteen
years for three attestations. One to qualification, one to
prerequisite knowledge and one to competence in
delivering care. Alas, the doors to employment had been
opened and the real work began. One more climb before a
plateau will at last appear.

All of it possible by an investment that produced a
monstrosity of debt, deepening the burgeoning, static
pressure to succeed, to not ever mess up.
Heavy and unseen, cutting off career paths and narrowing
manners of living to one methodology.
Despite its pervasiveness in affecting decisions, the burden
that the mind carried was most clearly understood some
years into working, when it's absence began to be revealed.
Ten thousand elephants that slipped off one by one until at
last he was able to lift high. Watching them splash into the
river valley below, couldn't help but wonder how he hadn't
crumbled under the weight.

Time after time, the final step across one finish line

dissolved into the first step over the new starting line.
Sometimes there was holiday and joy in between, other
times it struck through novel circumstances and
permanent shifts of reality.
Had they only been years of struggle through academic
systems it would have been sufficient, but it was still real
life.
Just below the surface, that's where it lives. A tempest that
can roar up and overtake without warning or explanation,
tenoring the motions that roam underneath.
Getting lost in fields of silver and gold while the waves of
life push the present past the way things used to be.

Growing in breadth and depth, losing linear advancement.
Futures removed just before he got there. Seemingly at a
long awaited destination but suddenly in the middle of
another journey within the journey.

Unjustifiable and unthinkable, as real as the hand on the
wall. A soul that received unwanted clarity on death, a
body that moved around the fog for years.
Not meant to be understood at the time, only dealt with
and shown acceptance by the continuance of breathing.
To himself, the totality of life sufficed for the supposition
of all questions and all answers, and in society the
ubiquitous self fulfilling aphorisms were given to console
the broken hearted. Reaching attempts at faith where
silence may be the best way forward, if only it can be given
an honest chance to be listened to.
How they could be so sure having been blindsided just as
he had, fumbling around time for meaning that seemed
devoid of any.
Everything happens for a reason, everything is going to be
ok. Indeed, what *was* that fabled reason everyone seemed

enamored with.   As if they had superseded his grief and been transformed into mystic priests.

The surety of that reason was not a certainty as believed, it was going to be revealed by what he made his life into as he transitioned into unknown seasons. An understanding brought about by actions that moved toward light and away from darkness.

Hoping the storms would cease one day, allowing sunshine to bring forth new life from the rain soaked earth. Casting a new world, a new person. Those were the ways he would bring truth to the prophecies, to redeem the sadness, to lay the foundations for all things yet to come.

Interlacing glass cascades sliced across the angled shoreline. pausing for a moment then retreating into phosphorescent reflections glowing with a golden pastel sunset, mauve washing over dazzling omnicolor, moving around the sky and disappearing into the copper sand below, becoming part of everything

trillions of water molecules danced over his neck and
shoulders, a splash of clear ocean that wet his hair and
laughed in his soul. bubbles shining with the brilliance of
sunlight, soft glitters bending fluid edges.
another glancing impact, then barely time for a breath
before the next wave came crashing overhead, sending
him twisting through turbid waters.

Spring Awakening

I

Since ever, Sceen's situational contemplations rooted in
virtuous constancy.
The most good for the greatest number had plenty of
successes but the recalcitrant idealism entrapped and
ensnared his naiveté as a need, a coping mechanism that
invited those who mistake kindness for weakness, onerous
consequences.
It took too many years before reaching the low point but
one day it hit him. Everything has been about everyone
else.
A slow moving sun opening behind clouds, remembrance.

A shift was initiated and from that point on not a thing to
worry about. It is happening.
Biologic form tasting the sweetness of life. A living
breathing spirit walking around in the world.

First generation ambition, making good on innate gifts and
ancestral sacrifice.
Paid his dues and jumped through hoops. Time and again,
more glass to bust through.
Ups and downs, tired and broken down, doesn't matter,
keep going.

Serenity was plainspoken and came without the mark of
calendar days. Once a year it was written.

Twenty-two years of pulling Atlas weight to catch a
glimpse of one long revered mountain top. The view was
majesty.
Pause a long moment and see bees buzzing across orange
white petunias, fungus breaking down a fallen pine tree.
Everything has a part, everyone plays their part.

Then a rapid loss of material fascination and a quick fall
back down to earth.

Audacious liaisons in extreme moderation tempered by
recklessness and good faith in youth. An innocent heart
that broke down and at last, broke through. On he drifted
into wisdom, stormy as ever, world vision had been created
and entered into.

familiarity made them look like circles but time opened a
spiral staircase, the upper stratospheres of mindspace

III

New presentations on theories of life purpose and
personal transformation are reintroduced into society all
the time but there is nothing new under the sun. Wisdom
is universal and nature is ancient. No secrets.

Stylistic verses can duplicate what can't be divided.
Attention on the pointed finger when it is the moon that is
shaping the tides.
In the end all are secondary to one question. Are you the
true expression of yourself. Are you staying true, are you
being real. Not to anyone or anything, to yourself.
Guidance and exploration can be academic or
entertainment but all discussion is prelude. No prologues
to being.

One must be absolutely certain that the starting point is a
heart of peace and love. A home to return to when there's
no place left to go.

IV

is it forced or does it flow
is your heart in it

(all action no talk is the way of the walk)

(not a flash a glow)

V

Meditate in the warmth of sunny mountaintops to feel the
grimy granulations of mud underfoot in the slums. Yes,
people live here.

Understand your language, faith and heart. Know the
words you need to hear, to pull you into cosmic humility
when you feel so small and without.
Know who is moving, understand why, then nothing else
matters. You are the very thing you are seeking.

VI

Show me you're not forgetting what it means, everything.
It can never be anything else unless you make it so.
Nobody can take it away but you.

It's your happiness, yours to carry with you.

Thought it all out thousands of times before so winky
congratulations on theoretical intellect. Now is time for
action.
Again, and again, then it just becomes what you do and
that becomes who you are.

What another may think, an obstacle to self expression.
Authenticity. Being who you are. It portends judgement
and rejection, trying to keep you from coming out into the
world. Sounds crazy but it's true.
Nonverbal cries, doublespeak and psycholinguistics gather
pointless meanings.

reach out, we could meet halfway

They are you and you are them but there is only one
person living in your reality, seeing it through the ways you
exist. That person is the creator.

VIII

Late one night, when the revelry of those who only come
out at night stepped down, he found himself in front of the
large framed bathroom mirror, dull brushed aluminum
with leaf stemmed flowers carved in golden bronze relief.
Images and style constructions, patterns and colors, a face
that changed around the same brown eyes. Leaning in.
Still looking and feeling so fresh. Unreal.
Eyes to eyes like times before but not interested in
observing.
Closer, into who was looking back into,
 veils presenting,

beyond it..

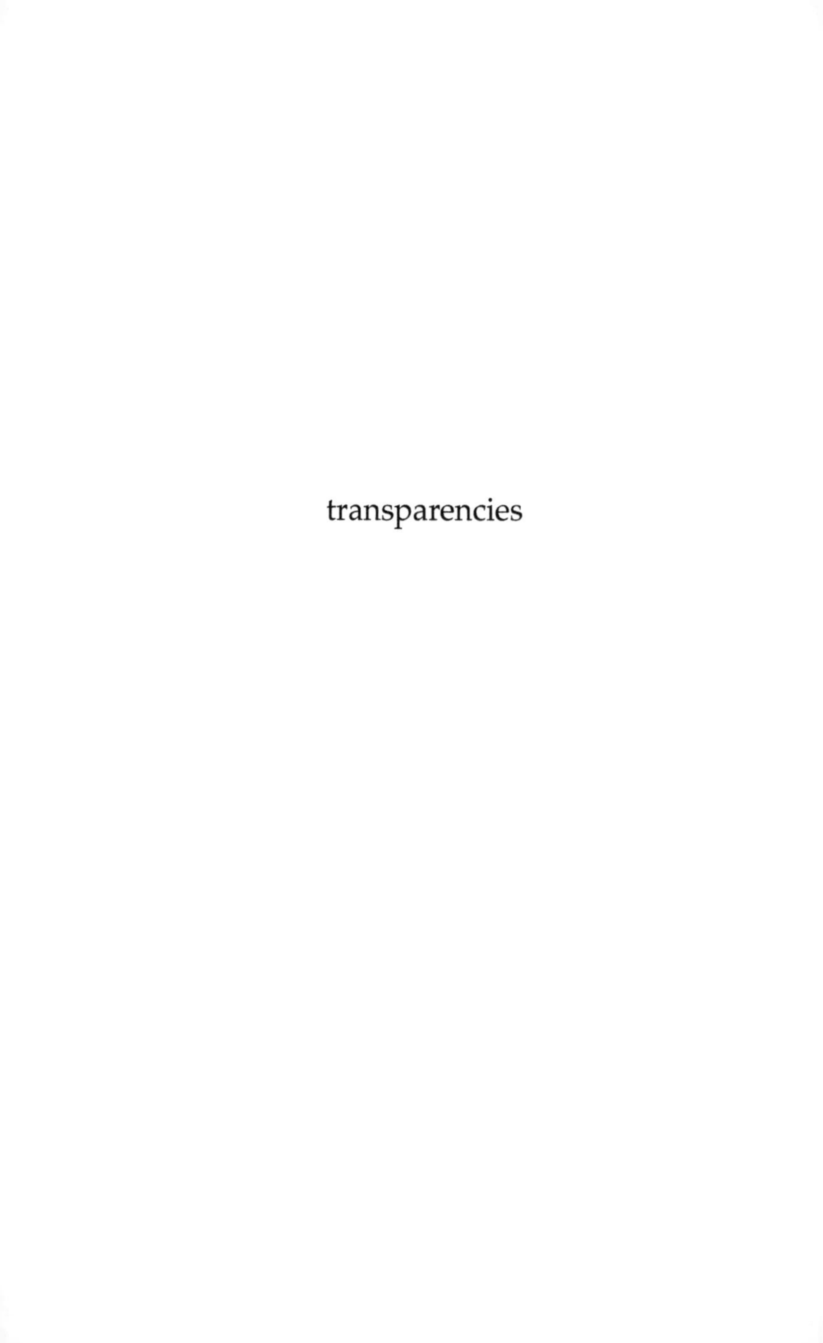

transparencies

something new, with choice and direction

take the chance while you can

I

First and foremost, before all the troubles with everyone
and everything else, it was time to be real and get real.
What exactly *has* he been doing all this time.

Choosing one over another. why, habit? laziness, or fear.
Are you all the things you think you think you are.

Presence and personal relations. Role and function in
home, family and society. Everything on the table and
nothing more important so nothing that can't be done,
won't be done, given up, sacrificed or banished.
Good bye, and thank you kindly, to the unconscious self
consciousness, entrapping nostalgia, groundless
sentimentality, empty cutsieisms, the exhausting fakeness
of being, hapless emotional tendencies of insecure
hurtfulness, ongoing drama, fanciful petrarchanism,
whimsical tiredness, thinly veiled diaphanies of vanity,
power shows, and even turning the shine down to keep
others in their blindness. The repressed, the pedantically

pugnacious, the distressed, the doubtful the pretense and
the surreptitiously spacey. A plain farewell to the old, the
tired, the overdone.

All the useless things in plentitudes and multitudes, they
have had their time if they have had any time at all.
Braids of time to the toil of memories, emotions left
discolored, opacified. Tarnished reflections of self coming
off the fragile shells of expectation. Gone on for too long
and can't move, can't free.
Leave them behind to forgive but never forget.
Let them fade away, let them go. Keep the true real, the
unity, all heart.

II

Separating darkness from light, seems easy, opens eyes
bright.
Exposure brings clarity and the months roll on as rivals
and adversaries are faced and battled. They weaken and
recede, then they come back so you tear them down again.
They find an opening, popping in to fill the mind until you
are lying in bed. Rising to greet you in the morning and
hanging around until you find the time, and see them
vanish into thin air.

Contrition may take a long time to work its way through
but the more time spent here now the less that will be
sacrificed again in the future.

III

Thoughts, though ephemeral and artful, hold their
dominance and influence as if they are the be all end all.
They're not, and neither are they imaginary things filtering
through. They have a physical home.
Electrical superstorms diffusing hormones and
neurotransmitters throughout the brain. Creating reality,
real as the rain falling from the sky.
Deeply connected pathways intertwining memories in the
swirls of the hippocampus, emotions in the curls of the
amygdala, the experiences of life in the systems of the
body.

The things you have always thought and the things you
know to be true.
Thousands of thoughts every day, rarely anything new.
Why so few.
Patterned, unconscious choices drawn from repeating
circumstances that have become part of what comes
naturally. Constituent and entrenched, running over the
same tracks, through the same paths.
Held in place so easy to follow, done it millions of times
without even knowing it. *It just happens.* One may want to
reevaluate the concepts of choice and ownership.

IV

Thoughts need to be slowed down and replaced, sparking
new passages, retraced and navigated, acquiring their own
steady and easy flow.

In the beginning, and for quite some time, motion in new directions is met with resistance that may seem impossible to overcome. Shifting the flow of trillions can be difficult, even in solitude.

V

Doors start to open and the hands that turn the pages of the story come into view. Past events, past actions. Influences on the development of style. Systems that took hold before the age of five. Second thoughts that led to the present.

You made a choice to the best of your understanding given the internal states of composure and the environmental conditions at the time, arrived at the consequences of that decision ever since, and here you are today. Now you've adjudicated over the present circumstances, wondering. When was the time to intervene so that the outcome would have been different. Was it the first decision nine years ago or the one four years after that. It's a blind romance with imagination because there is no telling which decisions were the most important or what would have led to what. Everything touches everything. When you arrive there's no way to know what you gave up or what could have been because you're not there to know it. Hence any lament may be misguided, no matter how honest or ideal it seems. Accept that you don't know.

VI

How to begin. Start, circles don't have endings. On to
interventions and the repetition of conscious choices.
Cannot be awake with one's eyes closed. Open them *wider*.
Not only the things you see and the people you meet that
are affected, that may affect and change back, it's also
biology, chemistry, physiology.
There are no shortcuts and there will be setbacks. Show
yourself love, no matter what you are thinking or what is
happening.

Forces in the world begging of one to go back,
uncomfortable emotions imploring, to please make things
easy. Not to cause any difficulties for yourself or for others,
not to bring about any trouble.

Old or new, them or you. What's it all worth to you. Stay
true.

An easily traveled, downward sloping jaunt to the poison
stream or rising through jungles of vines and overgrowth,
a green snake watches from a high branch.
The road less traveled in the mind emblazoned by double
sided machetes cutting through with the spirit of the soul,
breaking peace only for war.

dive in no matter how close excitement feels to fear

without any need to write, speak or think, instinct and
nature simple enough to understand.

VII

Look under covered overgrowth and ivies for a memory
that once was and no longer is. Rise without forlorn
foretellings of the past and tales of the future. All the
shoulds, woulds, never were and never will be. Where
your mind is that is where you are. Are you here.

Open eye scenes brimming under the silent hum of air
waves while two children share a sandbox under the
evergreen tree. They understand, do you?

it was never a choice between what is difficult and what is
easy,

being free in the mind

VIII

the past is past so do without placeholders for the way you
feel about what wasn't and what isn't.
given what's possible, now, what will happen.

one life to live

VIIII

Shock and trauma awe the mind, opening windows that
betray faith too easily. One can redeem a tragedy in
everlasting change, then breaking through. Surviving,
then finding a way to thrive.
For those with strength and energy, explorations through
meditation, study, and guidance can synthesize evolutions.
To the rest of time, *every passing moment is another chance to
turn it all around.*

X

All the dreadful things can be past in an instant.
You say goodbye to the things you should have never said
hello to and they're gone. You feel different, you are
different.

Awareness multiplies as the trappings of routine and rote
thinking are lofted into the present tense. The longer it
goes the more the connection in everything is revealed.
How one long awaited albeit minor shift works its way into
new ways seemingly unrelated. A better way of wellness
phases into relationships and vice versas, it's all together.
If old ways return it is too soon, preceded by thoughtless
invocations or worldly provocation. Let it slide by. Peace
follows then it reappears again. Identify it face it and place
it.

You hold on and you let go and then you hold on and then you let go again.

One day it fades away, a reminder to be self aware in the sacred space of mind.

Stay faithful as biochemical structures coalesce a metaphysical style.

Fatalistic determination. The next revolution will rise above the clouds. The sun is *always* shining.

The kingdom inside and the world in your mind.

Reality v. Truth

Nine senses, four dimensions, the vast unknown and unity.

Phantom chimeras of yesterdays' delusions dissipated as
he pressed his foot into the ground. The door behind is
closed and the road ahead is bright. The first step of a
journey that eternalized endings with beginnings.
Harmonious visions.
Winds that moved across the plain, streaming curves
rippling into waves of grass.

marvel and communion within Nature, places one can
never be alone

two dice lay atop glinting ivory marble
small black craters carving out the future in white gloss
embossment, ordinal numbers transposed through
cardinal addition
pickem up shakem up throw 'em up   click click jingle
knock bounce against the wall and like the tarot cards of
the oracle see them lay down, one by one

        Snake eyes   double Sevens

Sceen, *Rise* from this. Invitations and temptations from
devastation. The inescapable here.

Forlorn for unfamiliar memories, forage a way into past
intrinities and into a life worth living for. There is a path to
redemption. It started with a few steps, right before the
ground fell away, *remember*?
Everything learned, every realization every truth. You will
need them all through the ethers of time, each micron
forward ten thousand leagues deep.